Analyzing Labor Education in the Prophetic Books of Jeremiah and Lamentations

The Education of Labor in the Bible, Volume 16

Bible Sermons

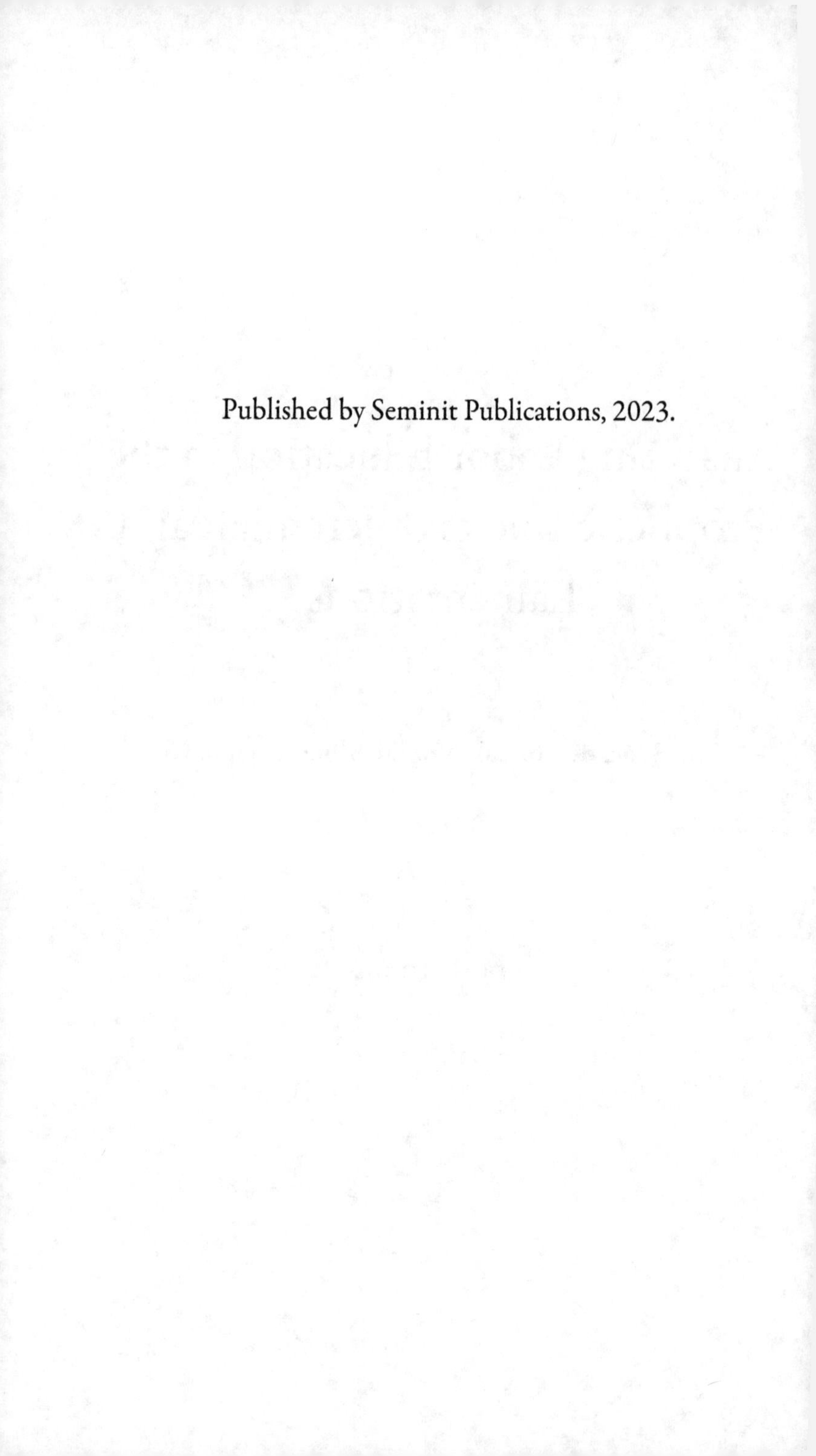

Published by Seminit Publications, 2023.

ANALYZING LABOR EDUCATION IN THE PROPHETIC BOOKS OF JEREMIAH AND LAMENTATIONS

First edition. August 7, 2023.

Written by Bible Sermons.

Table of Contents

Dedication

Jeremiah 2:14. *Is Israel a servant? is he a homeborn slave? why is he spoiled? The young lions roared upon him and yelled, and they made his land waste: his cities are burned without inhabitant. Also the children of Noph and Tahapanes have broken the crown of thy head. Hast thou not procured this unto thyself in that thou hast forsaken the LORD thy God, when he led thee by the way?*

The people of Israel had got into a dreadful state of poverty and famine and oppression. Their enemies had so destroyed the land that it was full of lions that even yelled in the very streets where once men and women and children abounded. And God says to them, «Is not this the result of your own sin? Was it so when you lived near to me? Have you not brought this upon yourself by your sin?» So, child of God, if you are unhappy tonight if you are mourning if you cannot find comfort in the world no comfort in God either, «hast thou not procured this unto thyself? When thou didst live near to God, when prayer was continual, when thou didst watch thy conduct, when thou didst go softly asking God to guide thee from day to day, was it not better with thee then than now. Then thy peace was like a river and thy righteousness like the waves of the sea. If it be not so now, hast thou not procured this unto thyself in that thou hast forsaken the Lord thy God when he led thee by the way?

— **Charles Spurgeon**

Introduction to the Book of Jeremiah and Lamentations

The basic theme of the book of Jeremiah is to measure the people's faithfulness to God in a difficult environment. God condemns dishonest practices in the same context in which he condemns idolatry and religious hypocrisy, making it clear that this prophetic book is not only about religious problems but also about social and ethical issues. Jeremiah is concerned with faithfulness in religious, family, military, governmental, agricultural, and all other spheres of life and work. As workers today, we face a problem similar to that of the prophet's time. We are called to be faithful to God in the workplace, but it is not easy to follow God's ways in many workplaces.

Jeremiah had to deal with the unfaithfulness of almost all the people. They were all unfaithful to the Lord, from the kings and princes to the prophets, and yet they generally came to the temple, offered sacrifices, and called on the name of the Lord, even though they did not acknowledge God in their way of life in all other respects (Jer **7:1-11**). They are the same as those who today attend church on Sundays and give their offerings, but live the rest of their lives as if God were not present.

Within the framework of faithfulness to God, the book of Jeremiah contains several passages directly related to work and many others that address the theme of faithfulness to God in all aspects of life, with clear implications for work.

Jeremiah does not present many new principles or commandments in his prophecies concerning work, but rather acknowledges those revealed in the earlier books of the Bible, especially in the Law of Moses. He rebuked God's people for not following the law and warned them that it would bring disaster upon them. When the disaster came, he taught them how to actually live God's law in their new - and depressing - situation. He also encouraged them with God's promise that He would eventually restore their joy and prosperity if they chose to return to faithfulness.

Although Jeremiah's words on work were spoken some six hundred years before the apostle Paul, they can be easily summarized in Colossians **3:23**: *"And whatever you do, do it with all your heart, as to the Lord and not to men"*.

Jeremiah and its Context

Many of us find our jobs problematic, at least some of the time. One of the striking aspects of the book of Jeremiah is that the prophet's situation was extremely difficult. His workplace (among the elites who ruled Judah) was corrupt and hostile to the work of God. Jeremiah was in constant danger, but he was able to see the presence of the Lord in the most difficult situations. His perseverance reminds us that it is possible to learn to experience God's presence in the most problematic workplaces.

Jeremiah grew up in a small town called Anathoth, three miles northeast of Jerusalem, the capital of Judah. Although geographically close, the two communities were very different culturally and politically. Jeremiah was born into the priestly line of Abiathar, but did not have much standing among the priests in Jerusalem. Centuries earlier, Solomon had removed Abiathar's authority (**1Ki 1:28-2:26**) and replaced him with the Zadok priestly line in Jerusalem.

When God called him to be a prophet in Jerusalem, Jeremiah found himself in the midst of priests who did not accept his inherited priesthood. Throughout his long career in Jerusalem, he was a suspicious and unpopular outsider. People who face cultural, ethnic, racial, linguistic, religious, or other prejudices in their current workplaces can identify with what Jeremiah faced every day of his life.

The Call of a Reluctant Prophet and the Description of the Role to be Fulfilled

———

In the thirteenth year of King Josiah's reign, in his early twenties, Jeremiah was called by God to be a prophet (Jer. 1:2). His task was to carry God's messages "*over the nations and over the kingdoms, to lift up and to pull down, to destroy and to overthrow, to build and to plant*" (Jer **1:10**). God's messages through Jeremiah were neither kind nor positive, for the Jews were disastrously close to ceasing to be faithful to God. Through Jeremiah, the Lord called them to return to Him before chaos erupted. As an outside consultant hired to reorganize the established order in a corporation, the prophet was called to change the established practices in the kingdom of Judah. Part of his task was to oppose the idolatry and evil practices that had become part of the worship here.

His prophetic work began during the good reign of King Josiah and continued through the reigns of the evil successors Jehoahaz, Jehoiakim, Jehoiakim, and Zedekiah, and during the total destruction of Jerusalem that occurred under the rule of the Babylonian Nebuchadnezzar in **586** B.C. During his four decades as God's prophet in Jerusalem, Jeremiah was constantly ridiculed and was a laughing stock among the city's inhabitants. In fact, he narrowly escaped several plots against his life (Jer **11:21; 18:18; 20:2; 26:8; 38**).

Jeremiah did not apply for the office of prophet, and we do not find anywhere in the text that he "*accepted*" God's call to be His spokesman. This is in contrast to the text of Isaiah, who, after his vision of God's holiness and majesty, heard him ask, "*Whom shall I send, and who will go for us?*" To which Isaiah replied, "*Here I am; send me*" (Isaiah **6:8**). When God told Jeremiah that he would be His spokesman in Jerusalem, the prophet protested because of his youth and lack of experience (Jeremiah **1:6-7**). However, God seemed to ignore this protest by immediately giving him prophetic messages for the people (Jer. **1:11-16**). Later, God also gave the new prophet instructions, a warning, and a promise:

Therefore, gird up your loins, get up, and tell them all that I command you. Do not be afraid of them, lest I make you afraid of them. Behold, I have set you this day as a fortified city, a pillar of iron and a wall of bronze against all this land, against the kings of Judah, their princes, their priests and the people of the land. "*They shall fight against you, but they shall not prevail against you, for I am with you*", declares the LORD, "*to deliver you*" (Jer. **1:17-19**).

Jeremiah knew from the beginning that his work as a prophet would be difficult. His task would pit him against the entire nation of Judah, from the king, princes and priests to the people in the streets of the city. But he received a clear call from God to do this difficult work, and he trusted God to guide him.

A General Overview of the Book of Jeremiah

The book of Jeremiah reflects the deteriorating situation in which the prophet found himself. At various times, he had the unenviable task of speaking out against the religious hypocrisy, economic dishonesty, and oppressive practices of Judah's leaders and their followers. Jeremiah was the voice of warning, the watchdog who called attention to difficult truths that others chose to ignore.

For thus says the LORD concerning the house of the king of Judah.... I will make you a desert like uninhabited cities. I will set destroyers against you. Many nations will pass by this city, and each will say to his neighbor, *"Why has the Lord done this to this great city?"* Then they will answer, *"Because they have forsaken the covenant of the LORD their God!"* (Jer **22:6-9**)

He was the pessimist who was actually the realist. Moreover, he was rejected and ridiculed by false prophets who insisted that God would never allow the city of Jerusalem to fall to an invader.

Jeremiah's persistence with his unwanted message for four decades is extraordinary; he simply did not give up on what seemed to be an impossible task. How many of us have given up in similar situations? Jeremiah's consistent faithfulness in following God's instructions is impressive in light of the relentless opposition and harsh criticism he faced. Although he was often called the "*weeping prophet*" because he mourned over the sin of his people and failed to convince them to return to *Yahweh*, Jeremiah's confidence never wavered. He knew that God, who had placed him where he was, would confirm the truth of his message. The prophet could be faithful to his unwanted calling because God had promised to be faithful to him. "*They will fight against you, but they will not overcome you, for I am with you*", declares the Lord, "*to deliver you*" (Jer. **1:19**).

In **605**, Nebuchadnezzar of Babylon attacked Jerusalem and carried off ten thousand of the most competent Jews (including Ezekiel and Daniel). At this time, Jeremiah's role expanded to bring the Word of God to the exiled Jews (Jer **29**). Among the captured Jews were false prophets who assured the exiles that Babylon's days were numbered and that God would never allow the inhabitants of Jerusalem to be captives, while Jeremiah warned them that they would be in Babylon for seventy years. Instead of acting on false hopes, the Jews settled in the land, built houses, planted gardens, gave their children in marriage, and stopped listening to the false prophets.

Meanwhile, the remaining inhabitants of Judah continued to reject God's message. In **586**, the Babylonians returned, sacked Jerusalem, tore down the walls, destroyed the temple stone by stone, and took the remaining able-bodied people as prisoners. Once again, Jeremiah's role changed (Jer. **40-45**). God kept him in the ruined city, which was briefly ruled by Gedaliah, to encourage the new governor and help the people understand what had happened and how to move forward in the midst of destruction. But once again, despite his pleading for them to hear God's message, they put their faith in a pathetic military alliance with Egypt, which Babylon quickly defeated. Jeremiah was taken to Egypt, where he died. In the end, the prophet had to endure both the stubbornness and refusal of the rulers to heed God's messages and the disaster that resulted. Prophets and Christians in the workplace may find that they do not have the ability to overcome all evil. Sometimes success means doing what we know is right even when everything is against us.

The last chapters (**46-52**) are mainly about the judgment God will bring on all nations, not just Judah. Although God used Babylon against Judah, Babylon would not escape punishment either.

In reading Jeremiah, one cannot help but be struck by the disastrous results of the persistent lack of faith on the part of Judah's leaders-the kings, the priests, and the prophets. Their lack of vision and their willingness to believe the lies they told each other led to the complete destruction of the nation and its capital, Jerusalem. The work that God gives us is serious business. Failure to follow God's Word in our work can cause serious harm to ourselves and to those around us. Leading the people of Israel was the job of the king, the priests and the prophets. The national disaster that soon overtook Israel was the direct result of their poor decisions and failure to fulfill their covenant responsibilities.

Topics Related to Work in Jeremiah's Book

The book of Jeremiah is not structured as a treatise on work. Because of this, themes related to work appear in different places in the book, sometimes separated by many chapters, and sometimes occurring together in the same chapter or passage. As far as possible, we will take these themes and passages in the order in which they appear in Jeremiah.

We have seen that Jeremiah's overriding concern is for the people to be faithful to God. As we move through the reading, we may see our work as an important area where God wants us to be faithful. If so, we will experience God's presence in our work. Therefore, our faithfulness to God and His presence in our work are related themes that we will return to often.

The Call to Labor (Jeremiah 1)

As we have seen, God prepared Jeremiah for the work of a prophet before he was born (Jer **1:5**), and at the right time He called him to that work (Jer **1:10**). Jeremiah faithfully responded to God's call to his work, and God gave him the knowledge he needed to do it (Jer **1:17**).

Although Jeremiah's calling was that of a prophet, there is no good reason to believe that the pattern of God's call, followed by a faithful human response and then God's provision for the work, is limited to prophets. God called and equipped Joseph (Genesis **39:1-6; 41:38-57**), Bezaleel and Aholiab (Exodus **36-39**), and David (**1 Samuel 16:1-13**) to serve as treasurer, chief builder, and king, respectively. In the New Testament, Paul says that God prepares all believers for work according to His purposes for the world (**1Co 12-14**). We can see in Jeremiah a pattern for all those who faithfully follow God in their work. As William Tyndale said long ago:

There is no work that can please God more than others: pouring a glass of water, washing dishes, being a cobbler, or an apostle, all are equal; washing dishes and preaching are equal, as far as action is concerned, in pleasing God.

God knows the ways in which we, like Jeremiah, are built according to His design. God guides us to use our skills and talents in godly ways in the world. We may not have the same calling as Jeremiah, and our calling may not be as direct, specific, and undeniable as his. It would be a mistake to think that our call to ministry should be like Jeremiah's. Maybe God was extraordinarily direct with Jeremiah. Perhaps God was extraordinarily direct with this prophet because he was so reluctant to accept the Lord's call. Either way, we can be confident that God will give us what we need to do our work, whatever it may be, if we are faithful to Him in the work.

The Kindness and Pollution of Labor (Jeremiah 2)

Long before Jeremiah was born, God declared that work was good for man (Gen **1**-**2**). As we said earlier, Jeremiah's method was to recognize what God had previously revealed and to point out how these principles were being put into practice-or not-in his day. In chapter **2**, Jeremiah spoke of how the people were perverting the goodness of the work. God said to His people, "*I brought you into a fertile land to eat of its fruit and its goodness; but you came and defiled My land and made My inheritance an abomination*" (Jer **2:7**). He added that the people had "*gone after things that have no profit*" (Jer **2:8**).

The Lord brought the people into a fertile land where the fruit of their labor would be abundant, but they rejected His presence by defiling His land. This is a standard expression of theological privilege in the ancient Near East: God created and owns the land, but He gave it to the people to be its stewards. God gave his people the great privilege of working his land, the place he had chosen for his temple, the place where his presence dwelt. Although the people of Jeremiah's day worked God's land with contempt, work itself was created by the Lord as a good thing. "*When you eat of the work of your hands, you will be happy, and it will be well with you*" (Ps **128:2**). Working the land is necessary and, when done in God's way, brings joy and a deep sense of God's presence and love. "*There is nothing better for a man than* *to eat and drink, and to say to himself that his work is good. I have seen that it comes from the hand of God*" (Eccl **2:24**).

But the work became polluted when people stopped being faithful to God in their work. They polluted the land because they stopped following God and "*went after vain things and became vain*" (Jer **2:5**). If our work is not going well, it may be a sign that our fellowship with God has weakened. Perhaps we have stopped spending time with God, perhaps because we are working so hard. Nevertheless, we are often tempted to try to fix the problem by spending more time on "*unprofitable*" tasks (Jer **2:8**), thereby neglecting fellowship with God even more. Our tasks are not unprofitable because we do not work long enough, but because without God in our work, it becomes fruitless and inefficient. What would happen if we got to the bottom of the problem and spent more time in fellowship with God? Could we anticipate with God all the important actions and decisions we will make during the day? Could we remember and pray for all the people we will meet? Could we review our work with God at the end of the day?

Recognition of God's Provision (Jeremiah 5)

Jeremiah lamented that "this people have a stubborn and rebellious heart; they have turned aside and gone astray" (Jer 5:23). It is God's land that they are stewards of, called to work it in the *"fear"* of the Lord. The *"fear"* (the Hebrew term yare) of God is often used in the Old Testament as a synonym for *"living in response to God. But Jeremiah warned that they were not aware of God as the source of the rain and the safety of the crops. "They do not say in their hearts, Let us fear the Lord our God, who gives the rain in its season, the autumn rain and the spring rain, and who keeps the appointed weeks of the harvest for us"* (Jer **5:24**). They are unfaithful because they imagine that they are the source of their own harvest (see Jer **17:5-6**). As a result, their harvest is no longer good. *"Your iniquities have turned these things away, and your sins have deprived you of good"* (Jer **5:25**).

This passage is one of many places in chapters **1-25** that speak of the "defilement" of the land: *"A dreadful and terrible thing has happened in the land: the prophets prophesy falsely, the priests rule by themselves, and my people are pleased with it"* (Jer **5:30-31**). In ancient times, when the economy depended primarily on agriculture, the pollution of the land was not only an aesthetic loss, but also a loss of productivity and abundance. It was also a rejection of the God who had given them the land. Chris Wright notes that the land-as well as a sacrament or a visible sign-is a thermometer of our relationship with God. Violation of the land (whether by corporations, armies, or individuals) denies that God owns it and that he has a purpose in making us his stewards.

The Success and Failure of Material Possessions (Jeremiah 5)

Does God deprive those who do evil in His sight of material success? Jeremiah is saying what some modern Christians would dare to say: God's lack of provision may be a sign that God does not approve of their work. God withheld the rain from Judah because of the sin of its people. *"Your iniquities have kept these things [the rains] from you, and your sins have deprived you of good things"* (Jer **5:25**). The prophet did not say that all cases of lack of provision or success are signs of God's judgment. This is one of the open questions that Jesus addressed almost six hundred years later when he said that the man who was born blind did not have this limitation as a sign of God's judgment (John **9:2-3**). Moreover, God provides material good even for those who are evil. According to Jesus, God *"makes his sun rise on the evil and on the good, and sends rain on the just and on the unjust"* (Mt **5:45**). From the book of Jeremiah we can only say that material success depends on God's provision, and that God can - at least sometimes - deny material success to those who practice injustice and oppression.

However, we must be careful not to jump to the conclusion that there is an absolute cause-and-effect relationship between our sin and God's punishment in all situations of lack of resources. Are the deprivations of the poor because they are wicked or lazy? Jeremiah would say that the poor lack resources because wicked or lazy people oppress them.

Injustices, Greed, the Common Good, and Integrity (Jeremiah 5–8)

Injustice in the World

Because they did not acknowledge God as the source of their bountiful harvests, the people of Judah lost all sense of responsibility before the Lord for the way they worked. This led them to oppress and deceive the weak and defenseless:

They exaggerate in works of wickedness; they do not plead the cause of the fatherless, that he may prosper, nor defend the rights of the poor (Jer **5:28**).

They cling to deceit, they refuse to return. I have listened and listened; they have spoken what is not right; not one of them repents of his wickedness and says, *"What have I done?"* (Jer **8:5-6**)

What should have been done for the good of all on God's earth was done only for the benefit of certain individuals and without fear of the God for whom they were to work. Therefore, the Lord withheld the rain from them, and they soon learned that they were not the source of their own success. There are parallels here to the economic crisis of **2008-2010** and its relationship to compensation, honesty in lending and borrowing, and the pursuit of quick profit even at the expense of others. It is important to avoid simplism, as today's major economic problems are too complex for the generalized principles we take from Jeremiah. Nevertheless, there is a connection-albeit a complex one-between the economic well-being of individuals and nations and their spiritual lives and values. Economic Well-Being is a Moral Issue.

Greed

GOD CALLS PEOPLE TO have a higher purpose than economic selfishness. Our primary goal is our relationship with God, within which provision and material well-being are important but limited issues.

Of you I remember the affection of your youth, the love of your betrothal, when you followed me in the wilderness, through a land not sown. Israel was holy to the Lord, the firstfruits of His harvest (Jer **2:2-3**).

Jeremiah looked around and saw that covetousness-the unbridled pursuit of financial gain-had supplanted love of God as the primary interest of the people. *"For from the least to the greatest they all seek gain; from the prophet to the priest they all practice deceit"* (Jer **8:10**). No one escaped Jeremiah's condemnation for covetousness. The prophet did not favor the rich or the poor, the small or the great. We see him go through *"the streets of Jerusalem"* to find at least *"one man, if there be any, that doeth righteousness, that seeketh the truth"* (Jer **5:1**). First, Jeremiah asked the poor, but found them hardened (Jer **5:4**). Then he spoke to the rich, *"but they, too, had all at once broken the yoke and the fetters"* (Jer **5:5**).

As Walter Brueggemann says, All people, but especially religious leaders, are blamed for their lack of principle in the economic realm...This community has lost all standards by which to judge and examine its insatiable and exploitative greed. Hearts have been inclined to get rich instead of fearing God and loving others. Whether of the rich (the king, Jer **22:17**) or the poor, such greed provoked divine wrath.

Working for the Benefit of Everyone

GOD'S DESIRE IS THAT we live and work for the benefit of others, not just ourselves. Jeremiah criticized the people of Judah for not caring for those who could not provide any economic benefit in return, including orphans and the needy (Jer **5:28**), aliens, widows, and the innocent (Jer **7:6**). This goes beyond the charges of disobeying specific parts of the law, such as theft, murder, adultery, false swearing, and worshiping false gods (Jer **7:9**). Jeremiah made this charge against specific individuals (*"there is wickedness in my people"*, Jer **5:26**), against all (*"all Judah"*, Jer **7:2**), against the leaders of business (the rich, Jer **5:27**) and government (the judges, Jer **5:28**), against the cities (Jer **4:16-18**; **11:12**; **26:2**; and others), and against the nation as a whole (*"this wicked people"*, Jer **13:10**). All components of society, individually and institutionally, had broken the covenant with God.

Jeremiah's insistence that our work and its fruits benefit others is an important foundation for business ethics and personal motivation. Whether an action contributes to the welfare of others is as important as the legality of the action. It may be legal to conduct business in a way that harms customers, employees or the community, but that does not make it legitimate in the eyes of God. For example, most businesses are part of a production chain that begins with raw materials to produce parts that become assemblies and then finished goods that enter the distribution system and reach consumers. Perhaps one actor in the chain has the opportunity to gain power over the others, squeeze the margins, and take all the profits. But even if this is done legally, is it good for the industry and the community? Is it even sustainable in the long run? It may also be legal for a union to preserve benefits for current workers by negotiating fewer benefits for new workers, but if all workers need such benefits, is the purpose of the union really being served?

These are complex questions, and we do not find a precise answer in Jeremiah. What is relevant in the book is that the people of Judah for the most part thought they were living according to the law, which probably included its many economic and labor regulations. For example, unlike some other prophets (e.g., Ezekiel **45:9-12**), Jeremiah does not mention that the merchants with whom he came in contact were using unjust weights and measures, which would have violated the laws of Leviticus **19:36**. However, God considered their economic and labor practices unfaithful because they followed the letter of the law but not the spirit. Jeremiah says that this ultimately did not allow all the people to enjoy the fruit of their labor in God's land.

Like the people of Judah, we all have opportunities to accumulate or share in the benefits we receive from our work. Some companies give most of their bonuses and stock purchase opportunities to top executives. Others distribute them widely among all employees. Some people try to take full credit for accomplishments in which they have participated. Others give as much credit as they can to their employees. Again, the issues are complex, and we should avoid making snap judgments about others. However, everyone can ask themselves a simple question: Does the way I use money, power, recognition, and other rewards from my job primarily benefit me, or does it benefit my coworkers, my organization, and my society?

Similarly, organizations can be guided by either greed or the common good. When a company uses monopoly power to charge high prices or uses deception to sell its products, it is acting in accordance with its greed for money. When a government uses its power to promote its own interests over those of its neighbors, or its leaders over its citizens, it is acting in accordance with its greed for power.

Jeremiah offers a broad perspective on the common good and its opposite, greed. Greed is not limited to gain that violates a particular law, but includes any kind of gain that ignores the needs and circumstances of others. According to Jeremiah, no one in his time was free from such greed. Is it any different today?

Integrity

THE WORD INTEGRITY means living by a single, consistent set of ethical values. When we follow the same ethical rules at home, at work, at church, and in the community, we have integrity. When we follow different ethical rules in different areas of life, we lack integrity.

Jeremiah laments the lack of integrity he sees in the people of Judah. They apparently believed that they could violate God's ethical standards in their work and daily lives and then go to the temple, act holy, and be saved from the consequences of their actions.

To steal, to kill, to commit adultery, to swear falsely, to offer sacrifices to Baal, and to go after other gods whom you have not known. Will you then come and stand before Me in this house which is called by My name and say, "*We are already saved*"; and then go on doing all these abominations? "*Has this house, which is called by My name, become a den of thieves in your sight? Behold, I myself have seen it*", declares the LORD (Jer **7:9-11**).

Jeremiah calls them to live in integrity, or their piety will mean nothing to God. "*And I will cast you out of my presence*", says God (Jer **7:15**). Our hearts are not right with God simply by going to the temple. Our relationship with Him is reflected in our actions, in what we do every day, including what we do at work.

Faith in God's Provision (Jeremiah 8:16)

In Jeremiah 5 we saw that the people did not recognize God's provision. If people did not recognize God as the ultimate source of the good things they already had, how much faith could they have to depend on God's provision in the future? John Cotton, the Puritan theologian, says that faith should be the basis of everything we do in life, including our work or vocation:

A Christian who truly believes ... lives in his calling by his faith. Not only my spiritual life, but even my civil life in this world and all that I live is through the faith of the Son of God: for him nothing in life is exempt from the unity of his faith.

Here again is the fundamental failure of the people of Judah in Jeremiah's day, their lack of faith. Sometimes Jeremiah expressed it as *"not knowing"* the Lord, which is a prerequisite for faithfulness. At other times he described it as not *"hearing"*-that is, not listening, obeying, and even giving weight to what God has said. At other times he has called it a lack of *"fear"*. But all of this is simply a lack of faith-a living, active faith in who God is and what He does or says. This lack taints people's view of work, leading to blatant violations of God's law and exploitation of others for selfish gain.

The great irony is that by relying on their own actions instead of being faithful to the Lord in their work, people ended up not finding the joy, satisfaction, and goodness of life. Eventually, God will deal with their lack of faithfulness and "*choose death rather than life for all the remnant that remain of this wicked seed*" (Jer **8:3**). God's laws are for our own good and are given to keep us focused on our right purpose. When we set aside God's laws because they prevent us from caring for ourselves in our own way, we reject God's plan for us and become the opposite. When we work by ourselves-and especially when we disregard God's laws to do so-the work does not achieve its proper purpose. We deny God's presence in the world. We think we know better than God how to get what we want. So we work according to what we want, not according to what God wants. However, this does not give us the good things that God wants us to have. Experiencing this lack, we engage in increasingly desperate acts of selfishness. We take shortcuts, oppress others, and hoard what little we have. Now we not only fail to receive what God wants to give us, but we also fail to produce anything of value for ourselves or others. If the whole community or nation acts in the same way, we will soon be at odds with each other, seeking less and less satisfying products of our labor. We have become the opposite of what we were meant to be as God's people. Now everyone "*recognizes and sees that it is evil and bitter to forsake the Lord your God and not to fear Me*", declares the Lord, the God of hosts (Jer. **2:19**).

The theme of abandonment of God, loss of faith in His provision, and oppression within the people is repeated at intervals throughout Jeremiah **8-16**. As a result, their prosperity disappears: "*The bellowing of the cattle is no longer heard; from the fowls of the heaven even the beasts have fled; they are gone*" (Jer **9:10**). As a result, they try to compensate for the loss by deceiving each other. *"Each one deceives his neighbor and does not speak the truth... Your dwelling is in the midst of deceit"* (Jer **9:5-6**).

The Role of Work in a Balanced Life (Jeremiah 17)

Jeremiah also focused on the cycle of work and rest. As always, the prophet began with God's previous revelation, in this case about the Sabbath rest:

And on the seventh day God finished the work that he had made, and rested on the seventh day from all the work that he had made (Gen **2:2**).

Remember the Sabbath day to keep it holy. Six days shall you labor and do all your work, but the seventh day is a Sabbath of rest to the Lord your God (Ex **20:8-10**).

But Jeremiah encountered a people who refused to keep the Sabbath:

This is what the LORD says: 'Beware of carrying a burden on the Sabbath and bringing it in through the gates of Jerusalem. Take no burden out of your houses on the Sabbath day, nor do any work, but keep holy the Sabbath day, as I commanded your fathers. But they did not listen, nor did they incline their ears, but stiffened their necks so that they would not hear or receive correction (Jer **17:21-23**).

Earlier, in the same chapter **17**, God spoke through Jeremiah and said:

Cursed be the man that trusteth in man, and maketh flesh his strength, and turneth his heart away from the LORD. He shall be like a bush in the wilderness, and shall not see good when it comes; he shall dwell in the rocky places of the wilderness, a salt land without inhabitant. Blessed is the man who trusts in the Lord, whose trust is in the Lord. He shall be like a tree planted by the waters, spreading its roots by the stream; it shall not fear in the heat, and its leaves shall be green; in the year of drought it shall not be afraid, nor shall it cease to yield its fruit. (Jer **17:5-8**).

Basically, Jeremiah was repeating his idea about faith in God's provision that we discussed in chapters **8** through **16**, using the Sabbath as a concrete example. When we rely on ourselves instead of being faithful to God, we believe that we cannot take time to rest. There is too much work to do if we are to be successful in our careers, homes, and hobbies, so we ignore the Sabbath to do it. But according to Jeremiah, if we rely on ourselves and make "*the flesh*" our strength, it will lead us into the "*wilderness*" as we relentlessly push ourselves **24/7** to achieve success. He will not "*see the good when it comes*". On the other hand, he who trusts in the Lord "*will not cease to bear fruit. In the end, it is counterproductive to ignore the need for a balance between work and rest*".

Work Blesses All Society (Jeremiah 29)

In Jeremiah **29**, the prophet emphasizes that God intends the work of His people to bless and serve the surrounding communities, not just the people of Israel.

This is what the LORD of hosts, the God of Israel, says to all the exiles whom I have sent into exile from Jerusalem to Babylon: "*Build houses and live in them, plant gardens and eat the fruit of them*". Take wives and have sons and daughters... multiply there and do not diminish. "*And seek the welfare of the city to which I have driven you, and pray to the LORD for it; for in its welfare you shall find welfare*". (Jer **29:4-7**)

This theme is found in earlier chapters, such as God's command not to oppress the aliens living within Judah's borders (Jer **7:6**; **22:3**). It is also part of the covenant that Jeremiah reminded Judah of. "*Abraham will become a great and powerful nation, and in him all the nations of the earth will be blessed*" (Gen **18:18**). Nevertheless, the false prophets in exile assured the exiled Jews that God's favor would always be with Israel, to the exclusion of their neighbors. Babylon would fall, Jerusalem would be saved, and the people would soon return home. Jeremiah tried to counter this false statement with God's true word to them: "*You will be in exile in Babylon for seventy years*" (Jer **29:10**).

Babylon would be the only home for that generation. God told the people to work the land diligently: "*build houses... plant gardens and eat their fruit"*. The Jews were to go forth as God's people, even though they were in a place of punishment and penance for them. Furthermore, the success of the Jews in Babylon was tied to the success of Babylon. *"Pray to the Lord for it [the city], for in its prosperity you shall prosper"* (Jer **29**:7). This call to civic responsibility from two thousand six hundred years ago still holds true today. We are called to work for the welfare of the whole community, not just our own interests. Like the Jews of Jeremiah's day, we are far from perfect. We may even suffer from our own lack of faithfulness and corruption. However, we are called and gifted to be a blessing to the communities in which we live and work.

God has called His people to use their many vocational skills to serve the surrounding community. *"And seek the welfare of the city where I have banished you"* (Jer **29**:7). It could be argued that this passage does not really prove that God is interested in the Babylonians. He simply knows that the Israelites cannot prosper as prisoners there unless their captors do as well. But as we have seen, concern for those who are not part of God's people is an inherent element of the covenant and appears in Jeremiah's earlier teaching.

Housebuilders, gardeners, farmers, and laborers of all kinds were specifically called to work for the good of all society in Jeremiah **29**. God's provision is so great that even when His people's homes are destroyed, families deported, lands confiscated, rights violated, and peace destroyed, they will have enough to prosper themselves and bless others. This will only be possible if they depend on God; hence the exhortation to pray in Jeremiah **29**:7. In light of Jeremiah **29**, it is difficult to read **1** Corinthians **12-14** and the other New Testament passages on gifts as applying only to the church or to Christians. (For a discussion of this point, see "*1 Corinthians*" in Teaching for the Work). God calls and empowers His people to minister to the whole world.

The Presence of God Everywhere
(Jeremiah 29)

This is not surprising, of course, since "*the earth is the Lord's and all that is in it, the world and those who dwell in it*" (Ps 24:1). God's presence is not only in Jerusalem or Judah, but even in the capital of the enemy. We can be a blessing wherever we are, because God is with us wherever we are. There in the heart of Babylon, God's people were called to work as if they were in the presence of God. It is hard for us today to understand how shocking this must have been to the exiles who had thought that God was only present in the temple in Jerusalem. Now they were told that they were to live in God's presence without the temple and away from Jerusalem.

The sense of exile is familiar to many working Christians. We are used to finding God's presence in the church, among His followers. But at work, alongside believers and non-believers, we may not expect to find God's presence. This does not mean that these institutions are necessarily unethical or hostile to Christians, but simply that their plans do not include working in the presence of God. Nevertheless, God is present and always seeking to reveal Himself to those who recognize Him there. When you settle in the land: plant gardens and eat what you produce, work and take home wages. God is there with you.

A Blessing for all Nations (Jeremiah 29)

Here we find an expanded view of the common good. Pray for Babylon because Israel's purpose is to be a blessing to all humanity, not just to itself: "*In you all the families of the earth shall be blessed*" (Gen **12**:3). In absolute defeat comes the time when they are called to bless even their enemies. This blessing included material prosperity, as Jeremiah **29**:7 makes clear. How ironic that in chapters **1-25** God deprived Judah of His peace and prosperity because of their lack of faithfulness, but in chapter **29** God would bless Babylon with peace and prosperity even in the face of the Babylonians' lack of faith in the God of Judah. Why? Because Israel's true purpose was to be a blessing to all nations.

This immediately calls into question any plan designed for the particular benefit of Christians. As part of our witness, Christians are called to compete effectively in the marketplace. We cannot run mediocre businesses and expect God to bless us while we underperform. Christians must compete with excellence on a level playing field if we are to bless the world. Any business organization, privileged relationship with suppliers, hiring preference, tax or regulatory advantage, or other system designed to benefit only Christians is not a blessing to the city. During the famines in Ireland in the mid-**19**th century, many Anglican churches provided food only to people who converted from Roman Catholicism to Protestantism. The ill will this caused is still reverberating one hundred and fifty years later, and it was simply an act of self-interest by one Christian sect against another. Imagine the far greater damage caused by Christians discriminating against non-believers, which fills the pages of history from antiquity to the present day.

The work of Christians in their faithfulness to God is meant to benefit all, beginning with those who are not part of God's people and extending through them to God's people themselves. This is perhaps the most profound economic principle in Jeremiah: that working for the good of others is the only reliable way to work for our own good. Successful business leaders understand that product development, marketing, sales, and customer service are effective when they put the customer first. Surely this is a best practice that should be recognized by all employees, whether they are followers of Christ or not.

The Restoration of Goodness in Labor (Jeremiah 30-33)

—

For twenty-three years, Jeremiah prophesied the coming destruction of Jerusalem (from God's arguments against Judah in chapters **2** through **28**). Then, in chapters **30-33**, the prophet showed his longing for the restoration of God's kingdom. He described it in terms of the joy of work without the corruption of sin:

Again I will build you, and you shall be built again, O virgin of Israel; again you shall take up your tambourines, and go out to dances with those who make merry. Again you will plant vineyards on the mountains of Samaria; the planters will plant them and enjoy them. For the day will come when the watchmen in the hill country of Ephraim will cry out, "*Arise, let us go up to Zion to the Lord our God*". (Jer. **31:4-6**).

Again, houses and fields and vineyards will be bought in that land (Jer. **32:15**).

The general context of the prophecies in Jeremiah is sin, then exile, then restoration, as we see here. Even the way she is called ("*virgin of Israel*") is a statement of restoration in comparison to Jer **2:23-25, 33** and **3:1-5**. Although the restoration of Judah was not yet imminent, the prophet spoke of the hope promised to the exiles in **29:11**. In the restored world, the people would continue to work, but although their work had been futile in the past, they would later enjoy the fruit. The life of the restored people would have the aspects of work, enjoyment, feasting, and worship all intertwined. The image of planting, harvesting, making music, dancing, and enjoying the harvest describes the joy of working while being faithful to God. This remains the Christian vision of the kingdom, partially fulfilled in today's world and completed in the new creation described in Revelation **21-22**.

Faithfulness to God is not a secondary issue, but is central to the enjoyment of work and its fruits. The "*new covenant*" described in Jeremiah **31:31-34** and **32:37-41** "*reiterates the importance of faithfulness.*

Behold, days are coming", declares the Lord, "*when I will make a new covenant with the house of Israel and with the house of Judah, not like the covenant I made with their fathers in the day I took them by the hand to bring them out of the land of Egypt, My covenant which they broke, though I was their husband*", declares the Lord; "*for this is the covenant I will make with the house of Israel after those days*", declares the Lord. I will put My law within them, and I will write it on their hearts; and I will be their God, and they shall be My people. And it will no longer be necessary for them to teach neighbor to neighbor, or brother to brother, saying, 'Know the LORD;' for all of them, from the least to the greatest, will know Me. (Jer **31:31-34**).

In one fell swoop, we see a restored world: the work of God's people enjoyed as it was always meant to be, with hearts faithful to the law of the Lord. People are restored to what they were always meant to be, working for the common good while experiencing God's presence in all aspects of life. Robert Carroll comments, "*The restored community is one in which work and worship are integrated*". Although we do not expect this to be a complete reality for us, since we are still in a world of sin, we can see some glimpses of such a scenario today.

The Emancipation of Slaves
(Jeremiah 34)

One of God's new commands in Jeremiah is the renunciation of slavery (Jer **34:9**). The Law of Moses required Hebrew slaves to be freed after six years of service (Exodus **21:2-4**; Deuteronomy **15:12**). Adults could sell themselves and parents could sell their children into slavery for six years. After that, they were to be freed (Lev **25:39-46**). In theory, it was a more humane system than modern serfdom or slavery, but masters abused it by basically ignoring the requirement to release slaves at the end of the term or to take back slaves for their entire lives for consecutive six-year periods (Jer **34:16-17**).

Jer **34:9** is significant because it called for the immediate release of all Hebrew slaves, regardless of how long they had worked as slaves. And even more drastically, it provided that *"no one shall hold a Jew, his brother, in bondage...so that no one shall hold them in bondage any longer"* (Jer **34:9-10**). In other words, it was the abolition of slavery, at least as far as Jews holding other Jews as slaves were concerned. It is not clear whether this was to be a permanent abolition, or whether it was a response to the extreme circumstances of military defeat and impending exile. In any case, it was not enforced for long, and the masters soon took back their former slaves as slaves. Nevertheless, it is an impressive economic breakthrough - or would have been if it had become a permanent measure.

From the beginning, God forbade involuntary and lifelong slavery among the Jews because *"you were a slave in the land of Egypt, and the Lord your God redeemed you"* (Deut. **15:15**). If God stretched out His arm to deliver a people, how could He bear for them to be slaves again, even to others of the same people? But in Jeremiah **34**, God added a new element: *"proclaiming liberty to every man his brother and every man his neighbor"* (Jer **34:17**). That is, the humanity of the slaves - referred to by calling them *"brother and neighbor"* - demanded that they be set free. They deserved to be free because they were - or should have been - beloved members of the community. This transcended religious or racial classification, for people of different religions and races could be neighbors to one another. It had nothing to do with being descended from the particular nation, Israel, that God had delivered from Egypt. Slaves were to be freed simply because they were human, as were their masters and the communities around them.

This basic principle still applies. The millions of people still enslaved around the world urgently need to be freed, simply because they are human beings. Furthermore, all workers-not just those bound to slave labor-should be treated as *"brothers and sisters and neighbors"*. This principle applies as strongly to inhumane working conditions, violations of workers' civil rights, unjust discrimination, sexual harassment, and a host of lesser evils as it does to slavery itself. What we would not subject our fellow human beings to, what we would not tolerate happening to our brothers, we must not tolerate in our businesses, organizations, communities, or societies. To the extent that

Christians can shape the environment in our workplaces, we have the same mandate as the people of Judah in Jeremiah's day.

Take a Firm Stand at Work (Jeremiah 38)

———

Most of what remains of the book describes Jeremiah's trials as a prophet (chapters **35-45**), his omens to the nations (chapters **46-51**), and the account of the fall of Jerusalem (chapter **52**). The story of Ebed-melech is a passage that stands out in the work. The story is simple: Jeremiah preached to the people while Jerusalem was besieged by the Babylonian army. His message was that the city would fall and that anyone who came out and surrendered to the Babylonians would live, but the officials of Judah did not take it as a motivational speech. With the king's permission, they put Jeremiah in a cistern, where he would starve during the siege of Babylon or drown in the next rain (Jer **38:1-6**).

Then a surprising thing happened. An immigrant named Ebed-melech, who was a servant in the royal palace, heard that Jeremiah had been put in the cistern. As the king was sitting in the gate of Benjamin, Ebed-melech came out of the palace and said to him, "*O king, my lord, these men have done wrong in all they have done to Jeremiah the prophet by throwing him into the cistern; he will die where he is because of the famine, for there is no bread left in the city*". Then the king commanded Ebed-melech the Ethiopian, saying, "*Take three men from here at your command and bring Jeremiah the prophet out of the cistern before he dies*" (Jer **38:7-10**).

It is very likely that the king's change of decision showed simple indifference in the matter (although God can use both indifference and activity on the part of a king). It is the unnamed Gentile slave (Ebed-melech simply means "*slave of the king*") who stands out as faithful. Although his immigrant status and racial difference made him a vulnerable worker, his faithfulness to God led him to speak out against injustice in his workplace. As a result, a life was saved. An anonymous gear on a lathe made the difference between life and death.

Ebed-melech's action on behalf of the prophet illustrated Jeremiah's message that faithfulness to God outweighs all other considerations in the workplace. Ebed-Melech did not know in advance whether the king would act justly or whether stepping out of the hierarchical chain would be a career-limiting move (or a move that would end his life, given what happened to Jeremiah). It seems that he trusted God to provide, regardless of the king's response. So Ebed-Melech was praised by God. "*Surely I will deliver you...because you have trusted in me,' declares the LORD*" (Jer **39:18**).

Jeremiah the Poet at Work: Lamentations

Although there is no evidence in the Bible itself that the book of Lamentations was written by Jeremiah, rabbinic tradition, the parallel themes in Jeremiah and Lamentations, and the eyewitness nature of the Lamentations point to Jeremiah as the most likely author of these five poems of woe. Judah and its capital, Jerusalem, were utterly destroyed. After a two-year siege, the Babylonians have taken the city, torn down its walls, looted and destroyed God's temple, and carried the able-bodied inhabitants into exile in Babylon.

Jeremiah is one of the few survivors left in the land, living among those who have clung to life during the famine and watched starving children die while false prophets continue to deceive the people about God's purposes. The book of Lamentations captures the desolation of the city and the despair of the people, while also pointing to the cause of that desolation.

Here we see the poet at work. In five tightly structured poems, he uses powerful imagery of the slaughter in the city as God allows His people to be punished for their heinous sins. But despite the emotional depth of his lament, the artist captures the devastation in a controlled poetic form. This is art in the service of emotional release. Although it is unusual for a discussion of "work" to include the work of artists, these poems force us to recognize the power of art to encapsulate the highs and lows of human experience.

The artist adds a note of hope in the midst of despair, rooting the future in the goodness of God:

This I bring to my heart, for this I hope: May the Lord's mercy never cease, for his goodness never fails; it is new every morning; great is your faithfulness! "*The Lord is my portion*", says my soul, "*therefore I hope in Him. The Lord is good to those who hope in Him, to the soul that seeks Him*" (Lam **3:21-25**).

For the Lord does not reject forever, but if He afflicts, He will also have compassion according to His great mercy. For He does not punish for pleasure, nor does He afflict the sons of men (Lam **3:31-33**).

Why should the living complain? Let them be courageous in the face of their sins! Let us examine and search our ways, and turn to the Lord; let us lift up our hearts in our hands to God in the heavens. (Lam **3:39-41**).

In the destruction of Jerusalem, the innocent suffered along with the guilty. Children starved, and faithful prophets like Jeremiah endured the same misery imposed on those whose sins brought about the city's destruction. This is the reality of living in a fallen world. When corporations collapse under the weight of bad decisions, gross negligence, or illegal practices, innocent people lose their jobs and pensions along with those who caused the disaster. At the same time, the injustices of this life are not eternal for Christians in the workplace. God reigns and His mercy never fails (Ps **136**). It is not easy to hold on to this divine reality in the midst of sinful systems and unprincipled leaders, but Lamentations tells us that *"the Lord will not be denied forever"*. We walk by faith in the living God, whose faithfulness to us will never fail.

Conclusion of the Book of Jeremiah and Lamentations

Through Jeremiah's trials and prophetic foreshadowings, the book immerses us in a captivating tale that culminates in the fall of Jerusalem. However, it is the story of Ebed-melech that shines like a beacon in the midst of this bleak picture. This humble immigrant not only defies the powers that be to save the life of the imprisoned prophet, but also demonstrates that even in the darkest of times, a small action can make the difference between life and death.

Ebed-melech's bravery and faithfulness are truly inspiring. Despite his vulnerability as a foreigner and subordinate worker, his devotion to God leads him to stand up to the prevailing injustices and fight for what is right. His intervention not only saves a single individual, but reveals the transformative power of a single person willing to act on his convictions.

In this fascinating story we find an impressive message: even when it seems imperceptible or insignificant in the eyes of the world, everyone can make a lasting difference if they dare to do the right thing. Whatever our situation or social status, we all have the potential to lead positive change and advocate for justice.

"Ebed-melech's story reminds us that our actions can change lives and transform adverse circumstances. We may never know how significant our impact will be until after the fact, but we must always remember that our actions have far-reaching consequences for both ourselves and those around us. In an increasingly indifferent world, we can be the voice that speaks out against injustice and the heart that is willing to help. Just as Ebed-melec saved a life, we too can make a difference in our environment and build a better future for all".

Don't miss out!

Visit the website below and you can sign up to receive emails whenever Bible Sermons publishes a new book. There's no charge and no obligation.

https://books2read.com/r/B-A-MZBS-VZPMC

BOOKS 2 READ

Connecting independent readers to independent writers.

Did you love *Analyzing Labor Education in the Prophetic Books of Jeremiah and Lamentations*? Then you should read *Analyzing Labor Education in the Prophetic Books of the Bible*[1] by Bible Sermons!

Discover the transformative power of labor education in the prophetic books of the Bible. In this fascinating book, we will explore practical teachings that we can apply to our day from a historical biblical context. Through captivating stories and powerful biblical quotes, you will discover key principles for professional success and the practical skills needed to excel in any work environment. You will learn how to maintain integrity

---

1. https://books2read.com/u/3LjPn7

2. https://books2read.com/u/3LjPn7

in the midst of pressure, make wise and ethical decisions, and find your purpose and passion in your work. We will learn how to maintain our integrity and positive influence in a challenging corporate environment. In addition, we will discover practical tips for developing our professional skills, managing stress, and finding satisfaction in our daily work.This is not just another book on education or professional development; it is a comprehensive guide based on sound principles drawn from the prophetic books of the Bible. If you are looking for a new perspective for your work life and desire to grow both personally and professionally from a solid and timeless foundation such as God's Word, this book is for you.*Get ready to be empowered by these practical teachings! Discover how you can succeed in your career while living according to God's purpose!*

Also by Bible Sermons

A Collection of Biblical Sermons
The Power of Great Gospel Words
The Power of Prayer: Men Ought Always to Pray
The Power of the Single Life in Christ
Analyzing The Power of a Life in Christ

Bible Characters Collection
Analyzing Biblical Scenes: 62 Inspiring Christian Teachings
from the Old Testament

Notes in the New Testament
Analyzing Notes in the Book of Matthew: Fulfillments of Old
Testament Prophecies
Analyzing Notes in the Book of Mark: Finding Peace in
Difficult Times
Analyzing Notes in the Book of Luke: The Divine Love of Jesus
Revealed

Analyzing Notes in the Book of John: John's Contribution to the New Testament Scriptures
Analyzing Notes in the Book of the Acts of the Apostles: A Journey of Continuation in the Work of Jesus

Overflying The Bible
Symbols in the Bible: Healthy Christian Doctrine
Bible Introduction: Overflying The Bible from Genesis by Brethren in the Faith
Chronological Prophecy: Things That Will Happen on Earth
Bible Study: Genesis 1. Creation in Six Days

Teaching in the Bible Classroom
Studying Teaching in the Bible Classroom: A Teacher's Guide

The Education of Labor in the Bible
Analyzing the Education of Labor in Genesis: The Purpose of Life on Earth
Analyzing the Teaching of Labor in Exodus: From Slavery to Liberation
Analyzing the Labor Education in Leviticus: The Spirit of the Law at Work
Analyzing the Labor Education in Numbers: Israel's Desert Experience for Today's Challenges
Analyzing the Labor Education in Deuteronomy: A Perspective on Working Life Today

God's Guide for Work: Discovering God's Will for a Particular Job

Analyzing Labor Education in Poetic Books

Analyzing Labor Education in the Prophetic Books of the Bible

Standalone

Analyzing Notes in the 4 Gospels: Commentary Biblical

Analyzing What is to Come: God's Prophecies

About the Author

This bible study series is perfect for Christians of any level, from children to youth to adults. It provides an engaging and interactive way to learn the Bible, with activities and discussion topics that will help deepen your understanding of scripture and strengthen your faith. Whether you're a beginner or an experienced Christian, this series will help you grow in your knowledge of the Bible and strengthen your relationship with God. Led by brothers with exemplary testimonies and extensive knowledge of scripture, who congregate in the name of the Lord Jesus Christ throughout the world.